Date: 2/27/12

J BIO JOHNSON
Orr, Tamra.
Chris Johnson /

CHRIS JOHNSON

Tamra Orr

Mitchell Lane

P.O. Box 196
Hockessin, Delaware 19707
Visit us on the web: www.mitchelllane.com
Comments? email us: mitchelllane@mitchelllane.com

Mitchell Lane

PUBLISHERS

Printing   1   2   3   4   5   6   7   8   9

A Robbie Reader Biography

Abigail Breslin
Adrian Peterson
Albert Einstein
Albert Pujols
Alex Rodriguez
Aly and AJ
AnnaSophia Robb
Amanda Bynes
Ashley Tisdale
Brenda Song
Brittany Murphy
Charles Schulz
Chris Johnson
Cliff Lee
Dakota Fanning
Dale Earnhardt Jr.
David Archuleta
Demi Lovato
Donovan McNabb
Drake Bell & Josh Peck

Dr. Seuss
Dwayne "The Rock" Johnson
Dwyane Wade
Dylan & Cole Sprouse
Eli Manning
Emily Osment
Emma Watson
Hilary Duff
Jaden Smith
Jamie Lynn Spears
Jennette McCurdy
Jesse McCartney
Jimmie Johnson
Johnny Gruelle
Jonas Brothers
Jordin Sparks
Justin Beiber
Keke Palmer
Larry Fitzgerald
LeBron James

Mia Hamm
Miley Cyrus
Miranda Cosgrove
Philo Farnsworth
Raven-Symoné
Roy Halladay
Selena Gomez
Shaquille O'Neal
Story of Harley-Davidson
Sue Bird
Syd Hoff
Taylor Lautner
Tiki Barber
Tim Lincecum
Tom Brady
Tony Hawk
Troy Polamalu
Victoria Justice

Library of Congress Cataloging-in-Publication Data
Orr, Tamra.
 Chris Johnson / by Tamra Orr.
    p. cm. — (A Robbie reader)
 Includes bibliographical references and index.
 ISBN 978-1-61228-064-6 (library bound)
 1. Johnson, Chris, 1985– —Juvenile literature. 2. Football players—United States—Biography—Juvenile literature. I. Title.
 GV939.J6127O77 2012
 796.332092—dc22
 [B]
                                                                              2011016777

eBook ISBN: 9781612281766

ABOUT THE AUTHOR: Tamra Orr is a full-time writer in the Pacific Northwest. She has written dozens of biographies of celebrities, sports figures, and other famous people. She is a graduate of Ball State University and an avid reader and writer. In her spare time, she enjoys camping and sleeping outside under the stars.

PUBLISHER'S NOTE: The following story has been thoroughly researched and to the best of our knowledge represents a true story. While every possible effort has been made to ensure accuracy, the publisher will not assume liability for damages caused by inaccuracies in the data, and makes no warranty on the accuracy of the information contained herein. This story has not been authorized or endorsed by Chris Johnson.

TABLE OF CONTENTS

Words in **bold** type can be found in the glossary.

Chris Johnson is known for speed and power. He also can jump when he needs to. Leaping over fellow player Kevin Mawae, he proves that nothing can stop this powerhouse player.

A Record-breaking Game

It was early in the fourth quarter against the Seattle Seahawks. The Tennessee Titans **running back**, #28 Chris Johnson, had the ball. He began running. No one was surprised. Although he had been with the Titans for only two years, Johnson was known for running and gaining yards on the field. He jumped over teammate Kevin Mawae. He gained four yards.

Four yards may not seem like much. It is, however, if you add those four to the other yards Johnson had gained over the rest of the year. When they were all put together, they totaled over 2,000. In the history of the National Football League (NFL), only five other players had ever been able to run that many yards in one season. These football greats

Johnson dives across the goal line after an incredible 62-yard run against the Seahawks.

include Eric Dickerson, Jamal Lewis, Barry Sanders, Terrell Davis, and O.J. Simpson.

Those 2,000 yards were incredible, and his amazing plays kept the crowd on the edge of their seats. Earlier in the game,

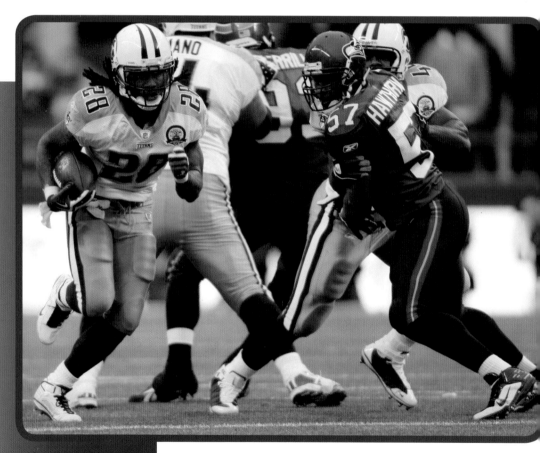

When Ahmard Hall (right) held linebacker David Hawthorne (57), a penalty was called against the Titans.

he ran 62 yards to claim the team's second **touchdown**. His teammates threw their arms up in excitement. Johnson was ready to do the touchdown dance, but then he spotted the flag. The **referee**, Ed Hochuli, had called a **penalty** (PEH-nul-tee). He cited Seahawk Ahmard Hall for **holding**, or grabbing a player who did not have the ball. The touchdown did not count, and neither did the yards.

Johnson was disappointed. He ran over to the sidelines for a short break, but his part in the game was not over.

With only four and a half minutes left, he scored a touchdown that won the game, 17 to 13. It was a huge win for the Titans, ending their season on a high note. Becoming one of the only players in NFL history to reach 2,000 yards was also a real victory for Johnson. As he told an ESPN reporter after the game, "It means a lot for me to get to 2,000 yards—only the sixth player ever to do it—and especially that we got the win today. I'm not really tired, just happy."

Johnson's days of running on the school track team have helped him speed over the field and race out of the reach of the other players.

The Two Titans

Not much is known about Chris Johnson's early life, before he discovered his passion and talent for football. He was born Christopher Duan Johnson on September 23, 1985, in Orlando, Florida. He went to Olympia (oh-LIM-pee-uh) High School. He was soon known there for his talent in sports. In fact, he was a football player for the Titans already—the Olympia High School Titans, that is. Little did he know that he would be playing for another Titans team years later, the NFL's Tennessee Titans.

At 5 feet 11 inches tall and 191 pounds, Johnson was known not just on the football field. He was also a successful **track** star. He scored some of the fastest times in the 100- and 200-meter runs of any other high school student in the nation. In fact, it was his speed on both the track and the football field that gained him the attention of NFL **scouts**.

The scouts noticed several other things about him. First, he had an amazing 35-inch **vertical** (VER-tih-kul) jump. In this test, players are asked to jump straight up in the air. It takes very strong legs to get that high. In the broad jump, players run and jump forward as far as they can. Johnson scored 10 feet, 10 inches. It was his score in the 40-yard **dash** that really got people's attention, though. He ran the distance in just 4.24 seconds. This was the fastest time ever recorded in the NFL.

It did not take long for college **scholarship** (SKAH-lur-ship) offers to start rolling in for Johnson. He decided to go to East Carolina University (yoo-nih-VER-sih-tee). Why? Most of the colleges that wanted him thought he should be the **cornerback** on the team. However, Johnson did not want to defend the **wide receiver** (ree-SEE-ver). He wanted to be a running back—the one who runs with the ball.

It is easy to understand why Johnson could have been a world track star instead of one of football's best players. He breaks speed records as he races over the ground.

Winning the Most Valuable Player award in 2007 was just another one of Johnson's achievements while playing for East Carolina.

Although East Carolina signed him as a wide receiver, they later moved him to running back.

"For me, it's just more of being a complete back, not just being able to run outside," Johnson explained to the *Los Angeles Times*. "You've got to be able to run inside too. That helps you prove everybody wrong, that you're nothing but a speed guy or a track guy."

It was time for Johnson to show off his football skills beyond his speed.

The Titans signed the lightning-fast Johnson in the first round of the

"Bolt of Lightning"

From 2004 through 2008, Johnson attended East Carolina University. He majored in **communications** (kuh-myoo-nih-KAY-shuns)—and cemented his **reputation** (reh-pyoo-TAY-shun) for speed on the football field. Each year, he played in nearly every game, making touchdowns and gaining more yards for the team. During his junior year, he missed spring training because he had neck surgery (SUR-jur-ee).

In 2008, as Johnson was finishing his senior year, the Tennessee Titans chose him during the very first round of the NFL draft. The Titans signed him for five years in a $12 million contract. Johnson played his first game for the Tennessee Titans on

At the draft pick, Titans head coach Jeff Fisher (far right) proudly presents first-round pick Johnson and second-round pick Jason Jones with their top-numbered jerseys.

September 7, 2008, against the Jacksonville Jaguars (JAG-wyrs).

His speed on the football field amazed everyone, including his teammates. Fellow running back LenDale White was a great partner for Johnson. Together they were called Smash and Dash. White was Smash for his power. Johnson was Dash for his speed. White liked the new player, saying that when Johnson

Smash and Dash made a great team out on the field. In the games against the Detroit Lions in 2008, both of them ran for over 100 yards and scored two touchdowns—each!—in the game.

joined the team, White "took a backseat to greatness."

By 2009, Johnson was named the NFL **Offensive** Player of the Year. Anyone tuning in to catch the Titans play knew right away that he was a player to watch. During the year, he made three touchdown runs of more than 85 yards each—incredibly long runs! He was the first player in NFL history to do this.

Phil Sims, a football expert on Showtime's *Inside the NFL*, had a lot to say about Johnson. He called him the team's "bolt of lightning." "All you have to do is watch him once to realize he's faster than anybody on the field," he said in 2009. "He's the fastest guy in the NFL. He's light on his feet. It's hard to get a big hit on him, and he's so light a lot of times he gets hit and it just pushes him a little to the side and he keeps going."

Sims was right. Johnson truly was unstoppable. What would he do next?

Johnson's joy for the game is clear—he loves what he does and he does

Part of the Team

Since 2009, Chris Johnson has been making victory a little bit easier for the Tennessee Titans. Between his speed and his skill, he scored 34 touchdowns in only three years. His teammates speak highly of him. "I'm just happy to be a part of it, to make history with him," **quarterback** Vince Young told *NFL Soup* in January 2010. "He's going to be a great player."

Former coach Jeff Fisher agreed. "He's young. He's special. He has the **potential** [poh-TEN-shul] to go the distance and change games . . . ," he said. "And you have to compliment him, because throughout the season, he practiced every single day. I think he took two days off the whole season. That's an amazing feat."

One of Johnson's biggest fans is, without a doubt, Johnson himself. He often refers to himself as "every coach's dream." He also believes that his running ability "has to make **defensive coordinators** [koh-OR-dih-nay-tors] not be able to sleep at night."

Over the past few years, Johnson has been given a number of awards and prizes. He has broken many records on the field, including the yardage record in that incredible game against the Seahawks in early 2010. Since 2009, he has also hosted the Old Spice Chris Johnson Football Camp at Battle Ground Academy (uh-KAD-uh-mee) in Franklin, Tennessee. More than 150 children between the ages of seven and fourteen come each year to learn about football from the pros.

In October 2010, Johnson and the rest of the Tennessee Titans were part of the Breast Cancer Awareness "Crucial Catch" Campaign. Game balls were decorated with pink ribbons, and players put on pink **cleats**, wristbands,

With each passing year, the number of trophies and awards Johnson is given grows. In 2010, he was named the Fed Ex Ground NFL Player of the Year.

Johnson is a true team player. He works well with his blockers, including David Stewart (76), Jake Scott (77), Kevin Mawae (68), Eugene Amano (54), Michael Roos (71), Alge Crumpler (83), and Ahmard Hall (45).

gloves, chinstraps, sideline caps, patches, and more. Even the field's goalposts were padded in pink.

What would be next for the Titans' bolt of lightning? His contract was scheduled to run out in 2013. No one knew what he had planned after that, but they knew whatever it was, it would be fast!

CAREER STATISTICS

Year	Team	G	ATT	RYDS	LNG	REC	RCYDS	RCLNG	TYDS	F	TD
2008	Titans	15	251	1,228	66	43	260	25	1,488	1	10
2009	Titans	16	358	2,006	91	50	503	69	2,509	3	16
2010	Titans	16	316	1,364	76	44	245	25	1,609	3	12
Career		47	925	4,598	91	137	1,008	69	5,606	7	38

(G=Games played, ATT=Rushing attempts, RYDS=Rushing yards, LNG=Longest run, REC=Receptions, RCYDS=Receiving yards, RCLNG=Longest reception, TYDS=Rushing + receiving yards, F=Fumbles, TD=Touchdowns rushing + receiving)

CHRONOLOGY

1985 Christopher Duan Johnson is born in Orlando, Florida, on September 23.

2004–2008 After graduating from Olympia High School in Orlando, Johnson goes to East Carolina University in Greenville, North Carolina. He plays football while studying communications.

2007 Johnson has neck surgery.

2008 He is drafted by the Tennessee Titans and plays in the first game of the season.

2009 He is voted Best Offensive Player by the NFL; he starts the Old Spice Chris Johnson Football Camp.

2010 He gains more than 2,000 yards over the season, a feat that only a handful of players have done before. He and his team participate in the Breast Cancer Awareness "Crucial Catch" Campaign.

2011 Johnson and Powerade teamed up for the 2010–2011 season for the Running Back to Schools program, which earns money for high schools. At $10 per yard, Johnson's 1,364 yards earned Nashville schools $13,640.

FIND OUT MORE

Books

If you enjoyed this book about Chris Johnson, you might also like these other Robbie Reader Contemporary Biographies:

Adrian Peterson
Larry Fitzgerald
Troy Polamalu

Works Consulted

Byrne, Kerry J. "Yo, Adrian: Titans' Johnson Stakes Claim as Best Running Back in NFL." *Sports Illustrated.com*, November 12, 2009. http://sportsillustrated.cnn.com/2009/writers/kerry_byrne/11/12/johnson.peterson/index.html

ESPN. "Johnson Ends with 2,006 Rushing Yards and Scores Winning TD for Titans." *ESPN.com*, January 3, 2010. http://scores.espn.go.com/nfl/recap?gameId=300103026

——. "Johnson Sixth to Rush for 2,000 Yards." *ESPN.com*, January 3, 2010. http://sports.espn.go.com/nfl/news/story?id=4793132

——. "Johnson Makes Fast Impression." *ESPN.com*, January 13, 2010. http://sports.espn.go.com/nfl/news/story?id=4821833

Farmer, Sam. "Chris Johnson Is Titans' Bolt of Lightning." *Los Angeles Times*, December 4, 2009. http://articles.latimes.com/2009/dec/04/sports/la-sp-nfl-farmer4-2009dec04

National Football League. "NFL Supports Breast Cancer Awareness Month with 'Crucial Catch' Campaign." *NFL.com*, September 29, 2010. http://www.nfl.com/news/story/09000d5d81af0979/article/nfl-supports-breast-cancer-awareness-month-with-crucial-catch-campaign

FIND OUT MORE

Parzych, Dan. "Titans RB Chris Johnson Teams Up with Powerade to Raise Thousands for Local Schools." *Titans Chronicle*, January 7, 2011. http://www.titanschronicle. com/2011/01/titans-rb-chris-johnson-teams-up-with-powerade-to-raise-thousands-for-local-schools.html/

Tennessee Titans Player Profile: Chris Johnson http://prod.static.titans.clubs.nfl.com/assets/docs/ Johnson_Chris_bio.pdf

Tennessee Titans Press Release. "Old Spice Chris Johnson Football Camp to Be Held June 15 in Franklin, Tenn." *Titansonline.com*, May 24, 2010. http://www.titansonline.com/news/article-1/Old-Spice-Chris-Johnson-Football-Camp-to-be-Held-June-16-in-Franklin-Tenn/27762557-15cc-45bd-9c36-457e578d975e

On the Internet

ESPN.com: Chris Johnson Profile http://sports.espn.go.com/nfl/players/ profile?playerId=11258

NFL.com: Chris Johnson Profile http://www.nfl.com/players/chrisjohnson/ profile?id=JOH127799

Sports Illustrated for Kids: Chris Johnson Profile http://www.sikids.com/football/nfl/players/8801/

GLOSSARY

cleats (KLEETS)–Shoes with spikes or studs on the bottom to give them extra grip.

communications (kuh-myoo-nih-KAY-shuns)–The field of spreading information, such as through radio, television, newspapers, or the Internet.

cornerback (KOR-ner-bak)–A football position between the linebacker and safeties for covering the outside areas.

dash (DASH)–A short, fast footrace.

defense (DEE-fents)–The team that is trying to keep the other team from scoring.

defensive coordinator (koh-OR-dih-nay-tor)–A coach in charge of the defensive players on a team.

holding (HOHL-ding)–Using one's body, especially the hands, to stop an opponent who does not have the ball from making a play.

linebacker (LYN-bak-er)–A defensive player who forms a second line of defense.

offensive (aw-FENT-siv)–On the side of the team that is trying to score.

penalty (PEH-nul-tee)–A punishment for breaking the rules of a game.

potential (poh-TEN-shul)–The ability to make something happen.

quarterback (KWAR-ter-bak)–The offensive player who calls the plays and throws the ball.

referee (reh-fer-EE)–A neutral person on the field who makes sure all the players are following the rules of the game.

reputation (reh-pyoo-TAY-shun)–The way a person's character is viewed by other people.

running back (RUN-ing bak)–A football player who advances the ball by running with it.

scholarship (SKAH-lur-ship)–Money that is awarded for someone to attend school.

scouts (SKOWTS)–People who go out to various schools to find promising athletes for a particular team.

touchdown (TUTCH-down)–A goal in football that is worth six points.

track (TRAK)–A sport that includes competitions performed on a track or running course, such as sprints, dashes, hurdles, and jumps.

vertical (VER-tih-kul)–Up and down.

wide receiver (ree-SEE-ver)–An offensive player whose main job is to catch passes.

INDEX